Here Comes Trouble

Written by
Larry Dane Brimner

Illustrated by
Pablo Torrecilla

Children's Press
A Division of Scholastic Inc.
New York • Toronto • London • Auckland • Sydney
Mexico City • New Delhi • Hong Kong
Danbury, Connecticut

For Taft Primary School
—L. D. B.

Reading Consultants
Linda Cornwell
Coordinator of School Quality and Professional Improvement
(Indiana State Teachers Association)

Katharine A. Kane
Reading Consultant
(Retired, San Diego County Office of Education
and San Diego State University)

Library of Congress Cataloging-in-Publication Data
Brimner, Larry Dane.
　　Here comes trouble / written by Larry Dane Brimner; illustrated by
Pablo Torrecilla.
　　　　p. cm. — (Rookie reader)
　　Summary: A young girl thinks that Wayne is a pest, until she gets to know
him better.
　　ISBN 0-516-22220-1 (lib. bdg.)　　　　　　　0-516-25968-7 (pbk.)
　　[1. Friendship—Fiction. 2. Stories in rhyme.] I. Torrecilla, Pablo, ill. II. Title.
III. Series.
PZ8.3.B77145He　2001
[E]—dc21
　　　　　　　　　　　　　　　　　　　　　　　00-047366

Here comes trouble.

What a pain!
Everybody else
calls him Wayne.

6

He likes to take
my favorite stuff.

Then he stacks it . . .

whacks it . . .

and treats it rough.

9

He takes it,

breaks it.

But just the good stuff.

I think he's nothing
but a pest.

Then Mom reminds me,
"He's your guest."

16

I think that means
I have to share.

I guess that's really
only fair.

I let him wear
my lucky cap. . .

and he gives me
a secret map.

We hunt.

25

We dig.

27

Then we play.

Can you come another day?

Word List (66 words)

a	fair	just	really	to
and	favorite	let	reminds	treats
another	gives	likes	rough	trouble
breaks	good	lucky	secret	Wayne
but	guess	map	share	we
calls	guest	me	stacks	wear
can	have	means	stuff	whacks
cap	he	Mom	take	what
come	he's	my	takes	you
comes	here	nothing	that	your
day	him	only	that's	
dig	hunt	pain	the	
else	I	pest	then	
everybody	it	play	think	

About the Author

Larry Dane Brimner has written dozens of books for children on subjects ranging from dancing dinosaurs to calendars. Noted books include *The Official M&M's® Book of the Millennium* (Charlesbridge, 1999) and *Snowboarding* (Franklin Watts, 1998), both IRA "Children's Choice" books, and *A Migrant Family* (Lerner, 1992), an NCSS/CBC "Notable Trade Book in the Field of Social Studies." Among his previous Children's Press Rookie Reader titles are *Cowboy Up!*, *Nana's Hog*, and *Dinosaurs Dance*. Larry digs for buried treasure in San Diego, California.

About the Illustrator

Pablo Torrecilla has been doodling and drawing ever since he can remember. When he was about five years old, he drew family portraits under his mother's den table. He grew up in Madrid, Spain. On weekends, he would visit his family's hometown where he loved the displays in the market, the smells, and the people. These became inspiration for his paintings and helped him to become an artist and illustrator. Now in California, he enjoys flying his kite at the beach, listening to music, and reading books in English, his new language.